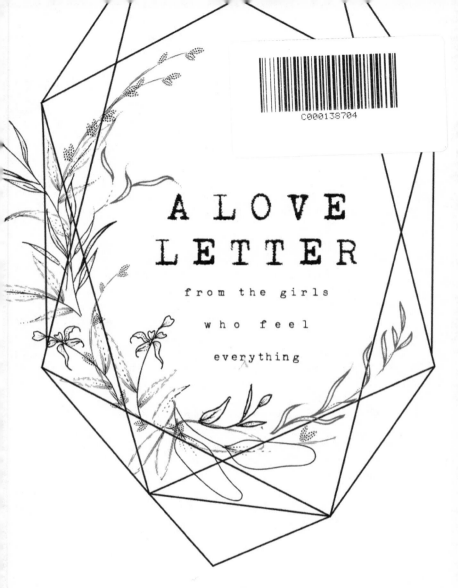

A LOVE LETTER

from the girls

who feel

everything

Poetry & Prose
by bestselling authors

Brittainy C. Cherry
and
Kandi Steiner

Introduction

Dear Reader,

It is with shaking hands and full hearts that we write this letter to you. In a time when texting is the most popular mode of communication, we want to take you back a few decades. Close your eyes and imagine, if you will, someone you care for deeply handing you a small, folded piece of notebook paper with your name scrawled lovingly across the top fold.

Can you see their handwriting?

Can you feel your cheeks heating, your smile splitting your face as you hold that sheet of paper close to your heart with a sigh?

We don't know how long it's been since you last received a love note. Perhaps it was in middle school, from the boy two desks over. Maybe it was while you were in the military, from the girl back home waiting for your return. Or, perhaps it was just yesterday, from someone you've loved for years — or someone you love only silently, not yet saying those three words out loud.

Whichever it may be, allow us to bring you into the following pages with warmth and understanding. We get it. In a time when feelings are shameful, when being the "cool girl" or "disinterested guy" is the goal, when admitting you feel anything other than indifference is a sign of weakness — we are your allies.

We are the girls who feel everything.

And this is our love letter. To you, to them, to us, to the world, to no one at all. Whether it's the brightest, sunniest day where everything is perfect, or the darkest, dreariest night of rain where life seems unbearable — we have lived it, we have survived it, and we have felt every, blissful, aching second.

Here's to embracing the feels, to the brave souls that listen to the way their hearts beat and aren't afraid to ask someone else if they feel those same beats, too. Here's to the girls, the boys, the love we sometimes share and the love we all-too-often conceal.

And more than anything, Reader — here's to you.

Love always,
Brittainy & Kandi

Maybe we should've spoken
while the coffee brewed each day.
Maybe we should've stated
the things that kept hurting us.
Maybe words would've helped
keep us from falling apart.
But maybe,
by mistake,
we simply forgot.

Forgotten Words
— B

You left my place, and I cursed out loud,
falling
to the floor
to the ground,
because you weren't supposed to matter
and suddenly
you were the only thing
I didn't want to put down.

Addiction
— K

If only you knew your worth wasn't
determined by the way he moaned as he
tasted your skin.

If Only
— B

I walk the tight rope,
heart beating
chest aching —
balancing on hope,

crashing on doubt.

To everyone around me
I am stable —
smooth as glass,
breathing soundly,

but inside, I shout.

Please don't fall —
left foot
right foot
capturing the eyes of all.

Breathe in, breathe out.

Anxiety's Circus
— K

I'd rather drown in
a million truths
than breathe in
one
dirty
lie.

Drowning
— B

In a time when dating isn't dating,
when loving makes you weak,
when the person who cares less
holds the most power,
and feelings are never spoken of...

How does the girl who loves openly
survive
against the boy
who never allows himself to love at all?

Survival of the Fittest
— K

Perhaps it wasn't a mistake,
yet merely a book that needed to
end.

Sometimes the final line
isn't as enchanting as the
opening.

Perhaps
— B

I fell into a dream last night,
and only then did I discover
that though I say that I'm okay,
I don't want you with another.

Waking Lies
— K

Even on your worst days:
When you can't control your thoughts.
When the tears come faster than your breaths.
When your mind lies to you and says you're worthless.

He'll stay.

The one who's meant for you will always stay.

If he doesn't:
Sweet baby.
Queen of all queens.

Let
Him
Go.

Even On
— B

Live boldly and unapologetically
and seek people who do the same.

Unapologetically
— K

What I Know About You
and How I Feel About You
are completely at odds.

Like the oldest of enemies
at war for reasons they can't remember
never a winner to be pronounced.

Enemies
— K

There doesn't always have to be a cage to
keep someone locked in.

Sometimes memories are the strongest
form of imprisonment.

Lock
— B

Love me, she begged.
I can't, he lied.
Why, she asked.
His silence was her only answer.

Answer Me
— K

When you look at me
you'll see that I am the light
that ignites my own way.

Light
— B

How wonderful,
the moment when you realize

Lost is not a place
or a tragedy
but a rare journey

a beautiful state
of Discovery.

Lost
— K

The world made me cold.
He made it his mission to thaw me.

Cold
— B

16

I knew you'd be better without me before you did.

Everyone thought you would fail,
but not me.
Because once I left,
you had to stand.
You had no other choice.

You couldn't sit and let me carry you anymore.
No, you had to stand.

And standing made you realize you wanted to walk.

Then you wanted to run.

And in the end,
I left so you could become a better man.
For another woman.
Who isn't me.

Better Man
— K

His words lingered,
gentle like the wind.

The whispers felt a touch like love,
yet his lips tasted more like sin.

Air
— B

If there is a way for you
to see me: the parts that burn.

Don't try to extinguish me.

Instead see
the heartbeats
within
the flames.

Fire
— B

He shows up in waves:
When I'm close to moving on.
When I almost let go.
When I see the shore.

Then he tries to
drown me.

Water
— B

I float back down to
solid ground.

You aren't the one for me.

No more blatant lies.
No more gaslighting.
No more promises of a future you've never dreamed of
achieving.

I face reality.

Earth
— B

She was patient
like the moon
perfectly content
waiting for the sun
that would illuminate
her shadows.

She had no patience
for the sun who tried
to eclipse her
for she had no desire
to be hidden.

She wanted to shine, too —
side by side.

Only then
would a sun's company
be better
than her own solitude.

Patience
— K

22

I don't want to lose you,
and so I lose
a little
of myself,
instead.

Because I want nothing more than to keep you
in the sheets you've always fled.

Choices
— K

How beautiful it is to be human.

That we can fall asleep
drowning
in tears
and pain

but wake to a new sunrise
on a new day
with a dry face.

The Human
— K

It was on the silent nights,
the ones she spent alone,
that she understood lonely was not the absence of
another
person,
but rather the absence
of self-love.

Lonely Girl
— K

When he thinks of me
I hope he remembers the sunsets
instead of the erratic storms.

Remember
— B

There is all this fear around being hurt. Hurt by feelings, by loving — knowing that love could be unanswered or worse, given and then taken away.

But why?

Is it not pain that we credit for our strength? Is it not hurt that peels back the layers to reveal our true self? Is it not in our weakest moments that we discover just how much we can endure?

I am not afraid of love, or the scars it may leave behind.

Those scars are proof that I have lived.

Scars
— K

It's pleasing to me
the way your heartbeats
kiss my ears.

Pleasing
— B

All this is easy
easy for him
him who I love
love that I know
know will kill me in the end
the end which is near
near to me he whispers
whispers empty words
words that make me feel
feel is what I shouldn't do
do I let him go?
Go, I said
said too late.

Go
— K

It's funny how love can come at bad times.
I wasn't ready for yours.
You were ready for mine.

I compared you to my others,
even though you were nothing alike.

Because of past hurts.
Because of past pains.
Because of a heart unhealed.

When you left, I knew I was the only one to blame.

But when I think of my favorite days
my mind always crosses over to
you.

You
— B

The elasticity of Time has always intrigued me.
How astounding it is that a moment in time can feel
like it occurred ages ago and like it happened only
yesterday all at once. Sometimes, Time is a friend,
a healer, a lover holding our hand as we walk
through hell. But other times, Time is an enemy,
bringing us back to a time and place that nearly
killed us, as if to just remind us that no matter
how strong we are now, we were once weak, we were
once broken, and we can be again.

Time
— K

One day she decided it was okay for her to feel.
She embraced the scars from the past and allowed
herself to fall apart.

In the morning, she cried into her coffee.
At night, she sobbed into her tea.

Sometimes one had to completely collapse for
their hearts to be freed.

One Day
— B

Isn't the saddest thing of all,
that love wasn't enough for me?

Enough
— K

Don't get for his attention.
That's not how love works.

Chase
— B

He called me beautiful.
He pulled my hair.
He whispered sweet nothings
into the air.
When my eyes faded,
he was still there.

When I awakened the smell of
his cologne was all that clung to the
pillowcase.

Pillowcase
— B

There is a riot within me
that wakes only once the sun has faded
and the night has become that all-encompassing,
shapeless,
heavy blanket around me.

I laugh freely
in the daylight,
but in the dark,
I am a slave to my anxiety.

Riot
— K

She's a summer soul trapped
inside a winter's freeze.

Misplaced Warmth
— **B**

Timing,
and Distance.
Friends,
or enemies,
depending
which lover
you ask.

Gray Area
— K

I missed him before he even left.
When I inhaled your perfume as he kissed my neck.
I loved him in part because he said he loved me too.
But how could he love me,
when his scent smells like you?

Smells Like You
— B

It was sick, really, the way I felt when he told me he couldn't love me. After months of being together, of sharing mind, body, and soul, he couldn't love me. And I should have been angry, and I should have been glad to be rid of him, but I was only sad. I was only hurt because I felt it was my fault. I'm not good enough, not interesting enough, not sexy enough.

I'm not *enough* for him.
One day he will love someone easily,
and she is not me.

It was sick, because it is such a privilege to be loved by me, to capture my heart the way he did, and yet I let him make me feel as if it was my fault he threw it away, like it was the diamond that was stupid instead of the diver who passed it up for rocks, instead.

Diamond
— K

I'm wild.
Erratic.
My hair doesn't always get brushed.
At times getting dressed is a chore.
I get sparks of inspiration.
Sometimes I don't sleep for days.

I work until my eyes cry,
and my chest burns.
I try to perfect imperfections.

Yet beside me he lays still.
Calm as can be.
He doesn't judge.
He doesn't scold.
He embraces my wilderness.

He remains unmoved by the beast within me.

Unmoved
— B

Yesterday it didn't exist.
Tomorrow it may be gone.
Yet in this moment,
we loved.

Moments
— B

It took me a long time, too long perhaps, to realize that I was strong enough to demand what I deserve. And once I did, once I learned the power of walking away when what I needed could not be given, I found that more peace comes from the pain of letting go than the ease of holding on.

Power
— K

Dreams filled her soul
like water fills the river —
gently
with the patience to
carve mountains
and the strength
to break levies.

Dreams
— K

If you knew how strong you were,
you'd never
doubt your heartbeats.

If You Knew
— B

I'm drunk
from your lips,
from your hips,
from the way you moan my name.

I'd forgotten what reality is as you stumble
through my dreams.
I'd forgotten to take a breath as you claim
my body as your masterpiece.

Pour another,
and let me show you
the way my skin feels
against your face.

Drunken Orgasm
— B

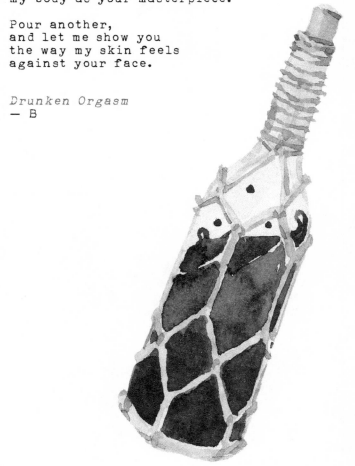

You are the moon and I the sun,
forever chasing.
We cannot be together without
one of us erasing
what truths lie within, of feelings and
thoughts untold.
Where your desire for love is shadowed,
mine is bright and bold.
So as you disappear again, leaving with
the dawn,
I ask myself which is worse: letting go,
or holding on?

Which is Worse
— K

Love me slowly.
Breathe me in.
Tell me I'm more
than all my worst sins.

How to Love the Scars
— B

I like doing things for the first time. I like that buzz, the excitement, the uncertainty. I like having expectations and love even more when they don't live up to reality. I like living life as if no two days are allowed to be the same.

My Favorite Things
— K

Oh, sweet love, can't you see?
It's not love if he only whispers
the words
when he's bent
between your knees.

Sweet Love
— B

In the middle of the night she awakened feeling shame
for all of the self-doubt
she fed herself each day.

She lay in the darkness
and imagined the light.

A breath, she took.
She closed her eyes.

Because no matter what
morning is promised
after every hard night.

Middle of the Night
— B

I'm not sad that I've lost you,
because the truth is I never did.
You're still here,
in my heart,
in my mind,
shaping the woman I'll be
when all the scars have healed.

Still Here
— K

I thought I knew what pain was,
but then you held me.

In my mind, so many thoughts came to life in that
moment —

How warm.
How safe.
How lovely.

You pressed a kiss to my forehead, a sigh leaving your
lips as you did, one that I read as content, but you
breathed as concern.

All you were thinking in that moment was,
"How much longer until I can leave?"

And I was there, too
in your arms
counting a hundred reasons you should stay.

In Your Arms
— K

The mask you wear each day
only scars you.

Mask
— B

I'm sorry.

I'm sorry for distracting you, my shoulders too bare, my thighs too exposed in these shorts.

I'm sorry for speaking too loud, my words ugly with truth, your ears sensitive from ignorance.

I'm sorry for chasing my dream, how selfish of me, to not ask for permission first.

I'm sorry for leaving you, how careless to stand on my own when you begged me to bend.

I'm sorry for proving you wrong, how embarrassing my smile is for you, I'm sure.

I'm sorry the flower you tried so long to drown bloomed anyway — that stem, once so fragile and weak, now roots dug deep.

I'm sorry that I was never sorry.

And that I never will be.

Sorry, Not Sorry
— K

When he makes you doubt yourself:
Your worth.
Your strength.
Your dreams.

Pack your bags and go.

Go
— B

One of the hardest lessons I have ever learned is that you can be the very best version of you, and still not be enough.

Lessons Learned
— K

Less fear
More love
Less confusion
More hope
Less heartbreak
More wholeness

Less you
More me

Less
— B

Walk away. No — run. Run from the things that do not serve you, the past that does not define you, the present that does not please you, and the people who do not value you. Trust me, peace is found in movement, in discovery, and the path is never-ending.

Run
— K

I used your name to
seal up the rips
in my heart.

I didn't know temporary stitches could
so easily be torn apart.

Your Name
— B

I am not the cool girl,
the one who is easy to like,
easy to love,
easy to leave.

I am the girl with the wild eyes,
the roaming heart,
the free spirit.

The tighter you hold on,
the more I long to flee.

Cool Girl
— K

Kiss me
like the setting sun kisses the water
on the horizon —
slowly,
gently,
and then all-consuming,
all at once,
swallowing me whole,
leaving us
in a hot new night.

Kiss Me
— K

He tried to treat me like a peasant.
I knew I was nothing less than a queen.

I left his side.

It wasn't a royal requirement
for a queen to have a king.

Royal
— B

Oh, silly boy. You must have mistaken her kindness for weakness, her love for a game, her heart for a toy. Until she walked away, a new scar on her skin and a smile on her face as she whispered, "Game over."

Games
— K

Every sunrise
you're allowed to
begin again.

Morning
— B

It is romantic
when lovers kiss with their eyes
and then with their hips.

Romance
— B

Defensive mode engages in 3...2...
All from a look
a question
a realization
of you.

3, 2, 1
— K

There will come a day
you'll walk alone
and you'll have to count your own
heartbeats.

Solo
— B

Those quiet nights when you hold me,
your heart beat under my ear,
your hands in my hair —
those are the times I hear it the loudest.

Those three words we haven't said,
but both know to be true,
waiting in a beautiful suspension
to be spoken.

I Love You
— K

Her insecurities were as loud as day,
but his gentle embrace made the noise stay at bay.

Pause
— B

There comes a point in your life
when you realize you were always enough.
It was the rest of the world
that was lacking.

A Point
— B

I saw our mistake.
Where you saw sunshine,
I only felt rain.

Mistake
— B

I long for mornings
waking wrapped up
in you,

hands between thighs,
tasting morning dew.

Morning Dew
— K

It's warm at night as the bodies fold.
Lust curls your toes,
feeding lies to your soul.
Yet when you wake up,
the bed's always cold.

Warm
— B

How tragic it is
that in order to love myself
I have to turn my back
on loving you.

Tragic
— K

In the middle of the night
you'll turn in your bed searching for him.
Longing. Craving. Begging.
Yet you'll remember that the ghosts of the past are best
kept buried away
because once morning comes their shadows always
burn.

Nightfall
— B

His eyes were the rope,
his kiss, the knot.
And the tree that I hang from,
grew from moments forgot.

The Hanging Tree
— K

We kissed in slow motion
and I allowed his lips to
l i n g e r .

Slow
— B

Before you,
Love was a noun.

It was flowers and titles,
pictures captured with true feelings somehow missed.
It was words screamed without intention,
promises made only to be broken.
It was a boy who treated a girl like nothing,
and a girl who allowed it.

After you,
Love is a verb.

It's doors pulled open,
arms held tightly as tears fall freely.
It's words whispered sweetly and genuinely,
brought to life by actions.
It's a man who treats a woman like everything,
and a woman who cherishes it.

Before and After
— K

Where worries disappear and your hands find mine.
Let's scroll around until the sun fades
and kiss the midnight sky with our dreams.

Walk with me.

The Walk
— B

I live for slow Sundays,
waking up under warm sheets
with your arms around me
my legs around you
our hearts wrapped up
in each other.

Sundays
— K

Still in my memories,
you'll always exist.

Still
— B

She was a moth
and he, the flame,
beckoning her closer,
promising comfort
and warmth.

She fluttered just close enough
to let him think she was his,
but kept enough distance
to safely fly away.

Because she soared with singed wings
as a painful reminder
of how that flame
could burn.

Singed Wings
— K

You plus me equals
endless
possibilities.

Math
— B

I handed you my heart,
this bloody, bruised, barely pulsing thing,
and you held it reverently,
eyes wide with adoration.
You wanted it for your own,
you vowed to care for it,
and for the first time,
I believed someone finally would.

The Gift
— K

He makes it easy to fall in love.

When he holds my hand and squeezes it so
gently.
When he holds my body and squeezes so tight.
When he's quiet. When he's loud.
When he kisses me hard and pins me to the
ground.

When my head rests against his chest,
and his fingers softly massage my neck.

When he looks me in the eyes,
and gives me that tiny grin.

Oh, how that smile owns me.

When he falls apart,
and still lets me in.

It turns out broken girls can fully be healed.
And he's living proof that true love is real.

He makes it easy.

Easy
— B

I fell for him in the unremarkable moments —
when he laughed a little too hard,
when he asked me which hat to wear,
when he sang a little off key,
when his hand found the inside of my thigh
as we drove down that country road.
It wasn't a grand gesture,
or an epic showcase of passion.
It was just existing in the same space with him and
realizing I could stay right there,
doing nothing particularly special,
and be blissfully happy for the rest of my life.

Grand Gesture
— K

Thank You

Reader,

As we bring this letter to an end, we hope you fold it and tuck it away in your pocket with a sense of renewal. It's our wish that you found a little piece of yourself within these pages, that your heart ached with a beat of understanding. And maybe — just maybe — you left a little piece of yourself within these pages, too.

The last note we want to leave you with is this: go forth and feel. Embrace your todays and tomorrows with love and passion, with the brave fearlessness it takes to not only acknowledge your feelings, but act on them.

Hug a stranger. Hug a friend. Text that boy — or don't, so long as you're being true to your heart and its desires. Kiss like it's the first time, or maybe like it's the last. Tell someone how you feel. Travel. See the world. Meet someone new. Let someone feel the way your heart beats, and ask them to let you feel theirs, too.

Write a love letter — and sign your name boldly at the bottom.

And above all else, take care of yourself. Because you're enough, and you're worth it.

You always have been.

Until next time, dear Reader.

Love always,
Brittany & Kandi

More from Brittainy Cherry

The Elements Series by Brittainy C. Cherry
All standalone novels with no interconnected characters.
Each novel is filled with heart-racing drama and love stories
that will make you hold your breath. Enjoy today!

The Air He Breathes

The Fire Between High & Lo

The Silent Waters

The Gravity of Us

Also by Brittainy C. Cherry
More novels filled with nothing but heart and soul. Fall in
love today with these angsty romances!

Loving Mr. Daniels

Art & Soul

The Space in Between

Our Totally, Ridiculous, Made-Up Christmas Relationship

Behind the Bars

More from Kandi Steiner

The What He Doesn't Know Duet
Charlie's marriage is dying. She's perfectly content to go down in the flames, until her first love shows back up and reminds her the other way love can burn.
#1 ➔ What He Doesn't Know
#2 ➔ What He Always Knew

On the Way to You
It was only supposed to be a road trip, but when Cooper discovers the journal of the boy driving the getaway car, everything changes. An emotional, angsty road trip romance.

A Love Letter to Whiskey
An angsty, emotional romance between two lovers fighting the curse of bad timing.

Weightless
Young Natalie finds self-love and romance with her personal trainer, along with a slew of secrets that tie them together in ways she never thought possible.

Revelry
Recently divorced, Wren searches for clarity in a summer cabin outside of Seattle, where she makes an unforgettable connection with the broody, small town recluse next door.

Black Number Four
A college, Greek-life romance of a hot young poker star and the boy sent to take her down.

The Palm South University Serial
Written like your favorite drama television show, PSU has been called "a mix of Greek meets Gossip Girl with a dash of Friends." Follow seven college students as they maneuver the heartbreaks and triumphs of love, life, and friendship.
#1 ➜ Rush
#2 ➜ Anchor
#3 ➜ Pledge
#4 ➜ Legacy

The Chaser Series

#1 ➜ Tag Chaser
She made a bet that she could stop chasing military men, which seemed easy — until her knight in shining armor and latest client at work showed up in Army ACUs.

#2 ➜ Song Chaser
Tanner and Kellee are perfect for each other. They frequent the same bars, love the same music, and have the same desire to rip each other's clothes off. Only problem? Tanner is still in love with his best friend.

About the Authors

Brittainy C. Cherry is an Amazon #1 Bestselling Author who has always been in love with words. She graduated from Carroll University with a Bachelor's degree in Theatre Arts and a minor in Creative Writing. Writing has been her passion for over fifteen years now, and she couldn't imagine doing anything else with her life. Writing her first book when she was 15 years old, she knew her career someday would surround the written word.

Brittainy lives in Brookfield, Wisconsin. When she's not writing happily ever afters, she is out in the world living her own happy endings. From concerts, to travels, she's always on a hunt for her newest adventure. If she's not finding a new place to see, she's probably playing with her adorable cats or visiting her loved ones.

CONNECT WITH BRITTAINY:

NEWSLETTER: BCherry Books Newsletter
FACEBOOK: facebook.com/brittainycherry
BOOKBUB: BookBub Updates
INSTAGRAM: Instagram.com/bcherryauthor
TWITTER: twitter.com/brittainycherry
WEBSITE: www.bcherrybooks.com

Kandi Steiner is a bestselling author and whiskey connoisseur living in Tampa, Florida. Best known for writing "emotional rollercoaster" stories, she loves bringing flawed characters to life and writing about real, raw romance — in all its forms. No two Kandi Steiner books are the same, and if you're a lover of angsty, emotional, and inspirational reads, she's your gal.

An alumna of the University of Central Florida, Kandi graduated with a double major in Creative Writing and Advertising/PR with a minor in Women's Studies. She started writing back in the 4th grade after reading the first *Harry Potter* installment. In 6th grade, she wrote and edited her own newspaper and distributed to her classmates. Eventually, the principal caught on and the newspaper was quickly halted, though Kandi tried fighting for her "freedom of press." She took particular interest in writing romance after college, as she has always been a diehard, hopeless romantic, and likes to highlight all the challenges of love as well as the triumphs.

When Kandi isn't writing, you can find her reading books of all kinds, talking with her extremely vocal cat, and spending time with her friends and family. She enjoys live music, traveling, anything heavy in carbs, beach days, movie marathons, craft beer and sweet wine — not necessarily in that order.

CONNECT WITH KANDI:

→ NEWSLETTER: bit.ly/NewsletterKS
→ FACEBOOK: facebook.com/kandisteiner
→ FACEBOOK READER GROUP (Kandiland):
facebook.com/groups/kandischasers
→ INSTAGRAM: instagram.com/kandisteiner
→ TWITTER: twitter.com/kandisteiner
→ PINTEREST: pinterest.com/kandicoffman
→ WEBSITE: www.kandisteiner.com

Kandi Steiner may be coming to a city near you! Check out her "events" tab to see all the signings she's attending in the near future:

→ www.kandisteiner.com/events

CPSIA information can be obtained
at www.ICGtesting.com
Printed in the USA
BVHW03s0847091018
529678BV00001B/224/P